Congressional
Research
Service

The National Flood Insurance Program: Status and Remaining Issues for Congress

Rawle O. King
Specialist in Financial Economics and Risk Assessment

December 10, 2012

Congressional Research Service

7-5700

www.crs.gov

R42850

CRS Report for Congress
Prepared for Members and Committees of Congress

Summary

On October 29, 2012, Hurricane Sandy struck the East Coast region, causing intense winds, high rainfall, waves, and storm surge, as well as economic disruptions in states throughout the Northeast and the mid-Atlantic region. Communities in New York, New Jersey, and Connecticut were particularly hard hit. The devastating floods exposed vulnerabilities in the region's public transportation and infrastructure and underscores the nation's growing exposure to coastal hazards. The full economic cost of Sandy will not be known for years, but current preliminary estimates of physical property damage, not including flood losses likely to be paid under the government's National Flood Insurance Program (NFIP), range from $30 billion to $55 billion, of which about $16 billion to $22 billion will be privately insured losses. Sandy is expected to require substantial federal disaster recovery assistance, including tens of billions for flood and hurricane protection and coastal restoration.

Given the geographic scope of heavily flooded areas and residential take-up rates (number of flood policies divided by total number of households) in affected coastal communities that participate in the NFIP, government payouts under the NFIP are estimated to be from $12 billion to $15 billion in flood claims. This amount exceeds the $4 billion in cash and remaining borrowing authority from the Treasury Department. The Obama Administration has announced it will ask Congress to raise the NFIP borrowing authority to $25 billion, or $4.025 billion over its current borrowing authority. But some experts have suggested a $30 billion borrowing cap would be needed to cover even higher projected losses. Emergency supplemental spending on disaster assistance comes at a time when Congress is considering spending cuts and tax increases to address the nation's fiscal debt.

In the wake of disaster clean-up and recovery along much of the East Coast region, policymakers, local officials, and other stakeholder groups have expressed a range of flood management concerns facing the NFIP. These include (1) escalating spending on federal emergency supplemental appropriations for disaster relief assistance; (2) uncertainty surrounding the NFIP's ability to reduce the nation's growing exposure to flood losses; (3) rising population growth and economic development in coastal watershed counties or floodplains areas exposed to hurricane-induced coastal floods; (4) persistently low insurance participation (take-up rates) in the NFIP; and (5) financing the cost of rebuilding communities stronger, more resilient.

On July 6, 2012, President Obama signed into law the Biggert-Waters Flood Insurance Reform Act of 2012, P.L. 112-141, that reauthorized the NFIP through September 30, 2017, and made a number of reforms to strengthen the future financial solvency and administrative efficiency of the program by raising historically low premiums and reducing homeowners' incentives for rebuilding in flood risk zones. However, several post-reform issues of contention remain for congressional consideration:

- revisions in the analysis and mapping of non-accredited levees;

- actuarial soundness, program solvency, and affordability;

- debt forgiveness;

- an integrated watershed flood risk assessment framework; and

- expansion of the private-sector role in flood risk.

This report provides an analysis of flood risk management, summarizes major challenges facing the NFIP, and outlines key reforms in the recently enacted Biggert-Waters Flood Insurance Reform Act of 2012. The report also identifies and presents some key remaining flood management issues for congressional considerations, and it concludes with a discussion of relevant policy options for the future financial management of flood hazards in the United States.

Contents

Figures

Tables

Appendixes

Contacts

O n October 29, 2012, Hurricane Sandy hit the East Coast region, flooding some coastal areas and causing massive economic disruptions in states throughout the Northeast and the mid-Atlantic region. Communities in New York, New Jersey, and Connecticut were particularly hard hit. In the wake of disaster recovery from Hurricane Sandy, policy awareness has refocused on the effectiveness of the existing unified national program for floodplain management in reducing the loss of life and property from weather-related coastal hazards (hurricanes, storm surges, and tornadoes), aging coastal protection infrastructure and increasing vulnerability to storm impacts, persistently low insurance participation in the National Flood Insurance Program (NFIP), and the escalating cost of flooding to taxpayers.

Despite billions spent on preparedness and structural[1] and non-structural[2] mitigation measures to reduce disaster-related losses, the nation faces growing exposure to flood-related losses. Some argue that a storm of Sandy's strength and intensity will occur more frequently, resulting in increasing incidents of major flooding and damage. This situation raises several policy concerns and questions: is federal flood insurance that complements land use management still a workable method of managing flood risk and reducing the costs and human suffering from floods and distributing burdens equitably among those who will be protected by flood insurance and the general public? Is flood risk still too risky for private insurers to underwrite? Could flood risk be effectively transferred to the private sector through reinsurance or to capital markets through catastrophe bonds? Should the NFIP debt to the Treasury be forgiven? Are the consequences of flood risks and the level of protection offered by hurricane protection systems well understood or communicated effectively to the public? These are some of the issues of contention that remain after recently passed NFIP-reform legislation in Congress.

This report provides an analysis of U.S. flood risk management policy, summarizes major challenges facing the NFIP, and outlines key insurance reform provisions in the Biggert-Waters Flood Insurance Reform Act of 2012.[3] The report also identifies and presents some key remaining flood management issues of contention for congressional consideration, and it concludes with a discussion of policy options for the future financial management of flood hazards.

Background

The United States is a geographically diverse nation exposed to hydro-meteorological (weather, climate, and water-related) perils that each year cause widespread physical and economic damage and threaten human life and fragile ecosystems. Already the most costly and prevalent natural disaster risk in the United States, incidents of flooding appear to be increasing.[4] The traditional method of flood hazard mitigation has been to build levees and other flood control structures to keep water away from population centers and agricultural areas. Beginning in the 1950s and 1960s, with the nation facing higher-than-expected flood losses from weather-related disasters

---

[1] Structural measures (levees, dams, floodwalls, channels modification) are those that change or control flood water flow to reduce the probability of flooding.

[2] Non-structural measures (flood-proofing, acquisition/relocation, and retrofitting structures) focus on floodplain management and flood warning to reduce risks associated with flooding and moving above and away from flood water.

[3] P.L. 112-141; 126 Stat 916.

[4] Testimony of Craig Fugate, Administrator of Federal Emergency Management Agency before the Senate Committee on Banking, Housing, and Urban Affairs, *National Flood Insurance Program Reform*, June 9, 2011, p. 3.

and breached levees, policymakers shifted focus from purely structural flood controls toward a system that included both structural and non-structural risk mitigation strategies.

The Regulatory Flood Management "Fix"

In 1968, Congress established the NFIP as a unified floodplain management strategy to reduce property losses from flood peril and public spending to compensate disaster victims. Today, the Department of Homeland Security's (DHS's) Federal Emergency Management Agency (FEMA) administers the program by developing flood hazard maps that are used to set flood insurance rates, regulating floodplain development, and informing those who live in the "100-year" floodplain of potential flood hazards.[5]

FEMA reports that the existing unified floodplain management strategy of mandatory flood insurance linked to floodplain management regulations saves the nation an estimated $1.6 billion annually in avoided flood losses.[6] Moreover, buildings constructed in compliance with NFIP building standards suffer approximately 80% less damage annually than those not built to NFIP standards.[7] But new social and economic issues of contention have arisen in the context of frequent historically extreme weather and climate events. These issues underscore challenges facing U.S. flood management policy that could require congressional oversight and possible regulatory reforms.

Issues of Contention

From a policymaker's perspective, the fundamental flood management challenge facing the NFIP is finding the best mix of strategies to reduce the nation's long-term exposure to flood losses while ensuring the program's solvency and statutory mandate to provide affordable flood insurance to the general public. These two policy objectives raise several broad post-reform policy questions:

- How can FEMA balance the program's fiscal soundness and actuarial rates with the affordability of flood insurance?

- How can the nation reduce the escalating cost of flooding and need for taxpayer-financed disaster assistance or weather-induced catastrophic floods?

- How to incentivize potentially at-risk property and business owners in coastal watershed counties or floodplain areas to purchase flood insurance protection while encouraging state and local governments to make appropriate land use adjustment to constrict the development of land in high risk flood zones?

---

[5] The financial management of flood hazards also involves (1) funding mitigation activities and (2) providing direct federal disaster assistance to individuals, private businesses, and communities to help rebuild destroyed property, provide temporary housing to displaced victims, and compensate uninsured victims. These costs are usually financed through emergency supplemental appropriations or dedicated disaster funds under the Robert T. Stafford Act.

[6] Testimony of Craig Fugate, Administrator of Federal Emergency Management Agency before the Senate Committee on Banking, Housing, and Urban Affairs, *National Flood Insurance Program Reform*, June 9, 2011, p. 2.

[7] Department of Homeland Security, Federal Emergency Management Agency, "National Flood Insurance Fund: Fiscal Year 2013, Congressional Justification," at http://www.fema.gov/pdf/about/budget/11h_fema_nfi_fund_dhs_fy13_cj.pdf.

- How can the private-sector's role be expanded in assuming NFIP flood risk?

Hurricanes Katrina and Rita (2005) and Sandy (2012) illustrate the potential cost and consequence of the nation's growing exposure to hurricane-induced coastal flooding and the tens of billions of tax dollars that would likely be spent on compensating flood victims and coastal reconstruction in the aftermath of storms. In this context, five issues are worthy of mention.

First, under the current flood risk management regulatory framework, residents who have a federally backed mortgage and live in a floodplain are required to have insurance against flood. However, these individuals often do not always purchase the mandatory insurance coverage. Estimates are that only 15% to 25% of at-risk properties in Special Flood Hazard Areas (SFHA) in the Northeast were insured for flood losses.[8] Only 38,785 residential and business policies were in force in New York City, as of August 31, 2012; and only 8,129 households and businesses in Atlantic City, NJ, had federal flood insurance coverage.[9] Nationally, recent reports suggest that only 18% of Americans in flood zone areas have flood insurance, which raised the possibility of high uninsured flood-related losses.[10] The transition toward full-actuarial rates could create an increasing financial burden on federal taxpayers who often fund emergency supplemental appropriations for disaster relief assistance.

Second, individuals tend to misunderstand flood risk, thinking that after a 100-year flood occurs, they are safe for another 100 years. Behavioral scientists have noted that many individuals in flood-prone areas often dismiss low-probability catastrophic events, misunderstand the risk-spreading function of insurance, and tend to be optimistic regarding the prospects of damage to their property.[11] The reality is that a 100-year flood only refers to a probability and that multiple "100-year" floods could occur in a row.[12] Some disaster experts believe a better way of portraying flood risk would be to refer to the 100-year flood in probabilistic terms as the 1% annual chance flood.

Third, NFIP insurance rates might not adequately reflect the actual risk. There is some anecdotal evidence which suggests that if property owners had to incur more of the cost of locating in flood-prone areas, they would make more efficient location decisions. One recent study suggested that NFIP's current rates are about a third of the true market-risk cost of flood insurance.[13] Congress established the NFIP with the statutory mandate that coverage be widely available and affordable. Rates are affordable because, unlike private insurers who are subject to state insurance regulatory requirements, the federal flood insurance program does not buy reinsurance or have to set rates to cover the cost of capital, taxes, and contingent reserves. The federal government serves as a direct primary insurer of last resort, diversifying (spreading) flood risk geographically

---

[8] Anita Lee, "Sandy Catches Northeasterners without Flood Coverage," *The Sun Herald*, November, 2, 2012, at http://www.weather.com/news/sandy-northeasterners-no-insurance-201211.

[9] Ibid.

[10] Susan Stellin, "Reconsidering Flood Insurance," *The New York Times*, November 8, 2012, at http://www.nytimes.com/2012/11/11/realestate/reconsidering-flood-insurance-after-hurrican-sandy.html?pagewanted=all&_r=0.

[11] See Howard Kunreuther and Paul Slovic, "Economics, Psychology, and Protective Behavior," *The American Economic Review*, vol. 68(2); p. 64-69.

[12] R.A. Pielke, "Nine Fallacies of Floods," *Climatic Change*, vol. 42(2), 1999, p. 413-438.

[13] Property Casualty Insurers Association of America, "True Market-Risk Rates for Flood Insurance," June 2011, at http://www.pciaa.net/web/sitehome.nsf/lcpublic/304/$file/NFIP_White_Paper_June2011.pdf.

through the mandatory purchase requirement and over time with the program's authorization to borrow from the Treasury.

Separately, FEMA's new digital flood maps might not meet certain flood hazard data quality standards.[14] For example, the maps do not adequately delineate areas of storm water and groundwater flooding or capture increases in localized storm water runoff flooding resulting from development, deforestation, and other land use changes.

FEMA recognizes this challenge and has undertaken many changes in its flood map assessment and mapping standards to accurately reflect risk on flood maps but more changes might be needed.[15] A potential reform could be to adopt a different regulatory standard of protection (and mandatory insurance purchase requirement), such as the 1-in-250-year or 1-in-500-year flood events, and to replace FEMA flood maps with those that contain high-accuracy and high-resolution land surface elevation data.

Adopting accurate flood maps that require new or sharply higher insurance premiums associated with greater risk exposure could cause unintended consequences that would require congressional oversight to ensure households and businesses are able to comply with the regulatory changes. Policymakers will likely be called upon to balance the presumed tradeoffs between keeping insurance affordable and widely available, as it has been since the NFIP's inception, and the regulatory changes needed to ensure the long-term financial viability of the NFIP. Driving debate surrounding this tradeoff is the reality of the large and growing segment of the U.S. population subject to the 1% annual chance coastal flood hazard[16] and the increasing frequency and severity of hurricane-induced floods.

Fourth, the increasing public cost of post-disaster recovery financing is another issue of contention that may merit future congressional oversight. Rebuilding of infrastructure like roads, bridges, and utilities in disaster-prone areas in the aftermath of Hurricane Sandy is expected to cost taxpayers tens of billions of dollars but an exact figure is still not known. Some experts have expressed concerns about taxpayer-financed rebuilding that duplicates the vulnerability that existed before Hurricane Sandy. The policy challenge will be to identify those disaster-prone areas that it no longer makes sense to rebuild (in light of future coastal hazards) and to develop a culture of resilience-building to reduce the nation's increasing flood risk vulnerability.

A related issue of contention is the notion that many at-risk property owners do not think flood insurance is a good investment or opt to finance post-disaster reconstruction with federal-disaster assistance, albeit insurance is generally considered the most effective way to finance post-disaster

---

[14] *The National Academy of Science*, "Mapping the Zone: Improving Flood Map Accuracy," 2009, at http://www.nap.edu/openbook.php?record_id=12573&page=13.

[15] FEMA, for example, shifted focus to coastal hazard mapping with its *Risk MAP 2010-2014 Multi-Year Plan*, March 2009, built on the Flood Map Modernization program. Risk MAP is an integrated flood risk management approach that weaves NFIP flood hazard data into watershed-based risk assessments that serve as the basis for local hazard mitigation plans and support community actions to reduce risk. As part of Risk MAP, FEMA has provided to communities New, Validated or Updated Engineering (NVUE) data for 54% of the miles mapped in the NFIP flood hazard inventory.

[16] FEMA estimated that about 8.7 million people or 3% of the U.S. population (based on the 2000 U.S. Census) live in Coastal AE Zones and VE Zones (i.e., areas subject to the 1% annual chance coastal flood hazard). See *An Estimate of the U.S. Population Subject to the One-Percent Annual Chance (100-year) Coastal Flood Hazard* by Mark Crowell and Kevin Coulton, Proceedings of Coastal Zone 09, Boston, Mass., July 19, 2009, at http://www.csc.noaa.gov/cz/ CZ09_Proceedings/Abstract%20PDFs/Oral.Crowell.pdf. A 2010 power point presentation of this study is found at http://www.norfma.org/conference/2010/090810_conf/090810/estimate_us_cooling.pdf.

---

recovery. The Biggert-Waters Flood Insurance Reform Act of 2012, P.L. 112-141, includes a provision to raise historically low premiums and reduce homeowners' incentives for rebuilding in flood risk zones. The key policy questions are as follows:

- Who should pay the cost of flood disasters?

- How to reduce the escalating costs of federal disaster assistance for flood damaged buildings and their contents?

- Are private markets ready to assume (underwrite or transfer to capital markets) a portion of the NFIP's flood risks?

Some critics point out that the costs—financial risk and ecological damage—are widely distributed to taxpayers across the country and the benefits, by contrast, are disproportionately enjoyed by wealthy counties and by owners of vacation homes.[17] However, not all beneficiaries of the NFIP are wealthy, and primary homes are also affected by the NFIP.

Fifth, hazard mitigation is considered an important element in reducing flood losses, but it is not always incorporated in risk management decision making at all levels of the government and in the private sector. For example, while local community officials might understand that for every hazard mitigation dollar spent five dollars are saved, the reality is that restrictive land-use zoning regulations and building requirements are not always enforced when such actions conflict with local plans for economic development. Moreover, the cost-sharing mitigation funding requirements on property buy-outs and relocation of at-risk properties and restoration of floodplains that provide benefits beyond flood control could be a financial burden for many local communities across the country already facing difficult budgetary choices. Many of these communities might also lack adequate financing to repair locally owned flood levee systems and, therefore, might not have them certified by the government as providing adequate protection against the 1% annual chance flood.[18] Without FEMA levee (or USACE) accreditation, the area behind the levee is mapped into a mandatory flood insurance purchase area.

Recent Developments

The Effect of Hurricane Sandy on the NFIP

On October 29, 2012, Hurricane Sandy struck the East Coast, causing massive floodwater inundation and economic disruptions in states throughout the Northeast and the mid-Atlantic region.[19] Sandy focused attention on vulnerabilities in the region's public transportation and infrastructure and on the nation's growing exposure to coastal flooding.

---

[17] See J. Scott Holladay and Jason A. Schwartz, "Flooding the Market: The Distributional Consequences of the NFIP," New York University School of Law, Institute for Policy Integrity, April 2010, at http://policyintegrity.org/documents/Floodingthemarket.pdf.

[18] See CRS Report R41752, *Locally Operated Levees: Issues and Federal Programs*, by Natalie Keegan et al.

[19] The states affected by Hurricane Sandy include Connecticut, Delaware, District of Columbia, Maine, Maryland, Massachusetts, New Hampshire, New Jersey, New York, North Carolina, Ohio, Pennsylvania, Rhode Island, Virginia, and West Virginia.

Given the geographic scope of heavily flooded areas and residential take-up rates (number of flood policies divided by an estimate of total households) in affected coastal communities that participate in the NFIP, government payouts under the NFIP are estimated to be from $12 billion to $15 billion in flood claims. This amount exceeds the $4 billion in cash and remaining borrowing authority from the Treasury Department for the program. According to media reports, the Obama Administration might be considering asking Congress to raise the NFIP borrowing authority to $25 billion, or $4.025 billion over its current borrowing authority. But some experts have suggested a $30 billion borrowing cap would be needed to cover even higher projected losses. Emergency supplemental spending on disaster assistance comes at a time when Congress is considering spending cuts and tax increases to address the nation's fiscal debt.

Table 1 provides a list of the top 20 flood events in the United States in terms of NFIP payouts. With expected insured flood losses exceeding $4 billion, Sandy could become the second largest flood disaster for the NFIP behind Hurricane Katrina, which was a pivotal event in the history of federal flood-control policy. Beginning with Hurricanes Katrina and Rita in 2005, and continuing through Hurricane Irene and Tropical Storm Lee in 2011, and Hurricane Sandy in 2012, public awareness has been focused on the destructive impacts of hurricane-induced coastal flooding.

Table 1. Top 20 Significant Flood Events Covered by the National Flood Insurance Program
(1978-August 31, 2012; $ nominal)

Rank	Event	Date	Number of Paid Losses	Amount Paid	Average Paid Loss
1	Hurricane Katrina	Aug. 2005	167,695	$16,265,032,023	$96,992
2	Hurricane Ike	Sept. 2008	46,412	2,663,374,853	57,385
3	Hurricane Ivan	Sept. 2004	27,653	1,587,147,757	57,395
4	Hurricane Irene	Aug. 2011	43,673	1,287,090,779	29,471
5	Tropical Storm Allison	June 2001	30,663	1,103,877,235	36,000
6	Louisiana Flood	May 1995	31,343	585,071,593	18,667
7	Hurricane Isabel	Sept. 2003	19,867	493,299,727	24,830
8	Hurricane Rita	Sept. 2005	9,509	472,397,546	49,679
9	Hurricane Floyd	Sept. 1999	20,438	462,268,248	22,618
10	Tropical Storm Lee	Sept. 2011	9,705	435,630,371	44,887
11	Hurricane Opal	Oct. 1995	10,343	405,527,543	39,208
12	Hurricane Hugo	Sept. 1989	12,840	376,433,739	29,317
13	Hurricane Wilma	Oct. 2005	9,616	365,167,555	37,975
14	Nor'Easter	Dec. 1992	25,142	346,150,356	13,768
15	Midwest Flood	June 1993	10,472	272,819,515	26,052
16	PA, NJ, NY Floods	June 2006	6,423	228,743,070	35,613
17	Torrential Rain – TN	Apr. 2010	4,108	227,962,140	55,492
18	Nor'Easter	Apr. 2007	8,637	225,731,111	26,135
19	Hurricane Fran	Sept. 1996	10,315	217,843,972	21,119
20	March Storm	March 1993	9,840	212,596,101	21,605

Source: U.S. Department of Homeland Security, Federal Emergency Management Agency.

Cost and Consequence of Recent Catastrophic Floods

Hurricanes Katrina and Rita in 2005 caused approximately $200 billion in economic losses, of which $21.9 billion related to insurance claims under the NFIP. Katrina financially overwhelmed the program. Then, in 2008, the Atlantic hurricane season was among the costliest on record for flood losses. Hurricane Ike alone caused about $2.7 billion in NFIP claims in coastal areas of Texas and Louisiana and further inland, including many areas not typically subject to tropical rain events. Extensive 500-year floods affected more than 11 million people in nine Midwestern states as major rivers in Illinois, Indiana, Iowa, Kansas, Michigan, Minnesota, Missouri, Nebraska, and Wisconsin overflowed their banks and levees. Especially hard hit states were Iowa, Indiana, and Illinois, where the river levels surpassed levels reached in the Great Flood of 1993.

It is the responsibility of FEMA to identify areas of special flood, mudslide or flood-related erosion hazards within communities, complete a Flood Insurance Study (FIS), and issue a Flood Insurance Risk Map (FIRM) showing the applicable risk premium rate zones. In the aftermath of Hurricane Katrina, FEMA focused on properly identifying properties facing residual risk behind levees and providing residents with adequate risk-based coverage. To ensure that FIRMs accurately reflected current flood hazards, particularly weather-related coastal hazards, FEMA began a nationwide FIS designed to remap the nation's floodplain. The FIS required FEMA to certify all levees appearing on FIRMs as meeting the 100-year protection regulatory standard. FEMA was able to produce digital flood hazard data for more than 88% of the nation's population and produce accurate flood hazard maps that reflected current flood hazards.

But the issuance of new or revised FIRMs posed a challenge for many families and communities remapped into Special Flood Hazard Areas (SFHA). This situation prompted widespread criticism about the accuracy of the underlying flood hazard engineering data and scientific methodology used in developing the FIRMs. During congressional debate that led to the passage of the Biggert-Waters Flood Insurance Reform Act of 2012, individual property and business owners, local officials and some Members of Congress representing areas remapped into a SFHA raised concerns about the accuracy of the maps, affordability of coverage, and sought to delay or avoid the implementation of the new or revised flood maps, in many cases making it easier to ignore flood risk.

Efforts to stall implementation of new or revised flood maps and mandatory purchase requirements was the political and regulatory environment in 2011 when Hurricane Irene and Tropical Storm Lee struck the Northeast and the nation experienced higher-than-normal rainfall and flooding in states along the lower Mississippi River Valley and the upper Midwest adjacent to the Missouri River not seen since the 1930s.[20] According to the National Oceanic and Atmospheric Administration's National Weather Service (NWS), there were 12 weather events that each caused at least $1 billion in damage.[21] Direct flood damages in 2011 totaled $8.41 billion.[22] To put this amount in context, flood damages in 2011 were 108% of the 30-year average (1980-2010) of $7.82 billion (adjusted for inflation).[23]

---

[20] These states include Arkansas, Illinois, Kentucky, Louisiana, Mississippi, Missouri, and Tennessee.

[21] National Oceanic and Atmospheric Administration, National Weather Service, "United States Flood Loss Report – Water Year 2011," at http://www.nws.noaa.gov/hic/summaries/WY2011.pdf.

[22] Ibid.

[23] Ibid.

The devastating flood damage following Hurricane Katrina in 2005, Midwest floods in 2008 and 2011, and Hurricane Ike in 2008 prompted legislative efforts in Congress to comprehensively reform and reauthorize the NFIP and transition the program toward a more resilient, sustainable, and comprehensive approach to flood management.

The Biggert-Waters Flood Insurance Reform Act of 2012

On July 6, 2012, President Obama signed into law the Biggert-Waters Flood Insurance Reform Act of 2012, P.L. 112-141, that reauthorized the NFIP through September 30, 2017. The law made a number of reforms to strengthen the future financial solvency and administrative efficiency of the program by raising historically low premiums and reducing homeowners' incentives for rebuilding in flood risk zones. See **Appendix B** for a summary of the major provisions in the new law.

Several post-reform issues of contention remain for possible congressional consideration.

- **Revised Analysis and Mapping of Non-Accredited Levees**. FEMA has agreed to assess and map residual risk (levee protection) below the 100-year standard that would give communities "credit" for levees that provide a level of protection less than the 100-year regulatory protection standard. There are inherent complexities and technical challenges in determining levee-specific risk (probabilities of flooding at a particular point in a levee) and establishing a corresponding risk premium.

- **Actuarial Soundness, Program Solvency and Affordability.** Insurance premium adjustments designed to strengthen the financial solvency of the NFIP could have an unintended consequence of property owners having to drop their policies because the premiums are not affordable. Public debate on the affordability issue will likely focus on the cost effectiveness and feasibility of implementing means-tested insurance premium increases that preserve some level of subsidization for low-income households.

- **Debt Forgiveness.** FEMA is currently obligated to repay about $17.5 billion owed to the Treasury Department from having to issue notes and other debt obligations to pay claims from Hurricane Katrina in 2005. Many insurance analysts believe FEMA will not be able to repay the current debt in the next 10 years.

- **Development of an Integrated Disaster Risk Management Approach.** Given the similarity in coastal and riverine hazard risks and water resources management challenges facing the nation, Congress may be called upon to decide whether the time has come for a comprehensive integrated watershed management framework of risk perception, risk management, and disaster strategy that goes beyond floodplain development management.

- **Private-Sector Role in Financing Flood Risk.** Is it feasible to have an expanded role of the private sector in assuming a portion of the NFIP's flood risk? Will private reinsurance companies be willing to assume primary insurer's flood risk and transfer it to the capital markets through alternative risk financing instruments?

A Nation Exposed to Flood Risk

Historically, flooding along river banks has been a major national public policy issue for which the government has played a substantial role as an insurer of last resort and a provider of disaster assistance to flood victims and communities. FEMA spends an average of $4.3 billion each year responding to a wide range of disasters.[24] These funds, which are intended to address immediate and longer-term impacts of disasters on individuals and communities, are in addition to the funds spent each year on compensation for flood victims for uninsured losses and mitigating future flood losses under the NFIP.

Statistical data from FEMA, the National Oceanic and Atmosphere Administration (NOAA), and private organizations suggests an increasing frequency of catastrophic flood events linked to extreme weather and climatic events like hurricanes, storm surge, or tornadoes. Urban populations and property assets and public infrastructure appear to be more vulnerable to coastal flood hazards and levee flood hazards. The nation arguably continues to face increasing exposure to flood risks as evidenced by the fact that floods that would historically occur once every 20 years are now projected to happen every four to six years.[25] Concerns have been raised that more than half of the U.S. population now live in coastal watershed counties or floodplain areas and approximately 50% of the nation's gross domestic product is generated in Gulf and Atlantic coastal areas.[26] One estimate from Lloyds of London and Risk Management Solutions (RMS) predicts that flood losses along the Gulf and Atlantic coastlines would increase 80% by 2030 with a one-foot rise in the sea level.[27]

Economic Regulation and Recovery from Flood Disasters

Congress has a responsibility through the "general welfare" and "interstate commerce" clauses of the U.S. Constitution to promote national economic growth. One factor affecting the nation's economic well-being is the proper functioning of markets for natural disaster risk. In deciding whether to intervene in private insurance markets, policymakers typically ask several questions: Do economic markets provide a sufficient amount of insurance against flood hazards? To the extent that flood insurance exists, are the insuring firms sufficiently capitalized so that widespread insolvency would not occur? Would federal disaster insurance crowd out private insurers and reinsurers and create unintended federal liabilities for taxpayers? Would insurers engage in "cherry-picking" the most appealing risks and leave the "less appealing" risk to the federal government?

---

[24] American Academy of Actuaries, "The National Flood Insurance Program: Past, Present ... and Future?, July 2011, at http://www.actuary.org/pdf/casualty/AcademyFloodInsurance_Monograph_110715.pdf.

[25] National Science and Technology Council, Climate Change Science Program and the Subcommittee on Global Change Research, *Weather and Climate Extremes in a Changing Climate - Regions of Focus: North America, Hawaii, Caribbean, and U.S. Pacific Islands*, June 2008, at http://www.climatescience.gov/Library/sap/sap3-3/final-report/sap3-3-final-all.pdf.

[26] U.S. Commission on Ocean Policy, "An Ocean Blueprint for the 21St Century," September 2004, at http://oceancommission.gov/documents/full_color_rpt/000_ocean_full_report.pdf.

[27] Lloyds of London and Risk Management Solutions, *Coastal Communities and Climate Change: Maintaining Insurability*, 2008, at http://www.lloyds.com/NR/rdonlyres/38782611-5ED3-4FDC-85A4-5DEAA88A2DA0/0/FINAL360climatechangereport.pdf.

The U.S. government has at times regulated private-economic activity for the purpose of promoting economic recovery and protecting or supporting particular economic groups. For example, economic uncertainty stemming from widespread flooding in the mid-1960s, the need for economic relief and recovery for flood victims, and calls for a reduction in the financial burden on taxpayers led to economic regulation of the nation's floodplains and insurance markets.

On September 9, 1965, Hurricane Betsy, a Category 3 hurricane hit the Louisiana coast, causing Lake Pontchartrain to overflow its banks and resulting in widespread flooding. Betsy was the first natural disaster to generate over a billion dollars in damages. At the time, there was little flood insurance because private insurers were unwilling at the time to offer protection to offset flood losses. In response, Congress created the NFIP in 1968 as a quid pro quo program that would regulate the nation's floodplains with land-use controls and building requirements that communities located in SFHA must adopt and enforce for property owners to be eligible for insurance under the program.

Under the NFIP, the government became a de facto regulator of certain economic activity in flood-prone areas. In the absence of a sufficient supply of insurance to meet societal demand, the government took action to safeguard the economic interests of consumers, private businesses, communities, and taxpayers. Economic regulation was accomplished in two ways. First, the government acted to address the cost and consequences of risky economic activity in flood-prone areas. Depending on whether a building is located in a government-designated SFHA, flood insurance may be required as a condition of obtaining a federally secured mortgage loan. Homeowners typically discover they need flood insurance during the home-buying process, which normally includes a disclosure of where the property is located relative to the SFHA that is mapped on a FIRM.[28]

Second, economic regulation was accomplished through "managerial regulation," with the government providing subsidized flood insurance for individuals and private businesses in communities that undertook specific steps to regulate the floodplain through land-use zoning ordinances and building standards.[29] The government later made the purchase of flood insurance mandatory for federally insured mortgages.

In general, there were four broad underlying causes for economic regulation—government intervention—in the market for flood insurance in the 1960s. *First*, people insisted that social and ethical values as well as economic values should be reflected in the operation of the economy. Persons suffering economic distress or dislocation from flood hazards sought and received governmental aid in dealing with their problem. The aid was in the form of disaster relief assistance, subsidized flood insurance, and government spending on flood risk identification and mapping.

Second, government action was viewed as being necessary to more efficiently coordinate and use resources. Economic regulatory programs were thought to be needed to prescribe certain land-use zoning ordinances and building-code standards to govern economic or business behavior to reduce the physical and economic risks associated with coastal hazards.

---

[28] Properties not financed by federally insured or guaranteed mortgages usually fall outside of the NFIP's insurance regulatory framework. Although there is no requirement to purchase flood insurance to protect the property as collateral, the property owner might be subject to land-use development and zoning and construction ordinances.

[29] James Anderson, "Economic Regulation," *Encyclopedia of Policy Studies*, Stuart S. Nagel, ed. (New York: Dekker Publishers), 1994, p. 404.

Third, as the nation experienced widespread flooding in the 1960s, people became interested in shifting some of the risk from themselves to government. In response, policymakers changed the way economic risk of flooding was defined and the means of achieving security for the individual. Disasters, whether man-made or natural, were initially considered inevitable or "acts of God" but came to be viewed as public problems that required government action to protect individuals, businesses, communities, and taxpayers. Government assistance in the form of subsidized insurance premiums was viewed as a solution to reduce the future costs and risks of investing in flood-prone areas.

Premium subsidies were initially considered necessary because residents in flood-prone areas often did not understand the flood risk when they built in floodplains (flood maps were not available), there were no public safeguards restricting construction on the floodplain, and premium subsidies on pre-FIRM structures could provide an incentive for local communities to participate in the program and discourage unwise future floodplains construction. Premium subsidies were intended to be phased out over time as the number of pre-FIRM properties gradually diminished when they were damaged and rebuilt or relocated under stronger floodplain management and building codes.

Fourth, sole reliance on insurance markets for flood risks was not an option. This situation provided a rationale for possible government intervention in the economy to ensure that the costs of living in flood-prone areas were not ignored. Individuals and insurers at risk of flooding, however, have in the past lacked the information necessary for the market system to operate effectively. Insurers did not always have flood hazard maps, as they do now, and thus had no reliable, consistent, and cost-effective way to identify and assess flood risk. Homeowners did not (and sometimes still do not) have the information needed to make rational economic decisions about real estate investments. All this resulted in a misallocation of resources that required and still arguably requires government intervention to protect the public interest.

Financial Management of Flood Risk

Flood hazards are deemed commercially uninsurable in the private-insurance market given that only those most exposed to loss tend to purchase coverage, the possibility of catastrophic losses, and concerns about the insurer's ability to correctly price the contracts of insurance because of limitations in hazard assessment. Traditional insurance principles indicate that financial intermediation through insurance contracts tend to work best when the insurer is able to gather a large enough pool of independent risks to allow the actuarial technique of "law of large numbers" to diversify the risk. Because the nature of flood risk is that many property owners simultaneously face the same flood hazard when the event occurs, their risks tend to be highly correlated—not independent. Correlated risks means the insurer must charge higher premiums to reflect a larger risk load or administrative costs that accounts for the uncertainty faced by the insurer in predicting future losses of the pool. The premium level that private insurers needed to adequately underwrite flood hazards would be so high that few would be willing to purchase coverage.

The NFIP was a public-policy response to the flood peril and escalating costs of taxpayer-funded disaster relief for flood victims. Government mapping of areas prone to flooding, subsidized flood insurance, and floodplain management regulations were key to the program's structure and function.[30] Federally backed flood insurance was made available to homeowners and businesses

---

[30] 42 U.S.C. § 4001(a); § 4012(a)-(b).

in communities that voluntarily agreed to adopt and enforce floodplain management ordinances designed to reduce flood-related property losses. The creation of the NFIP marked a significant shift in U.S. flood control policy. The shift was away from a "levee-only" flood reduction approach toward a risk identification, risk financing, and floodplain management approach that was intended to foster individual responsibility and build local self-sufficiency in terms of land-use zoning ordinances and construction standards.

Federal flood insurance was considered to be an economically efficient way to indemnify flood victims and to have them internalize some of the risk of locating property in the floodplains.[31] The federal government would use its capacity to spread losses over time with the NFIP's ability to borrow money from the U.S. Treasury to offset program deficits. A federal government insurance program, it was thought, could also link the availability of flood insurance to land-use regulation and building codes that would, in theory, reduce long-term flood risk.

The NFIP has undergone major changes largely in response to significant flood events over the years. As an illustration, the program was created after Hurricane Betsy devastated the Gulf Coast in 1965. After Hurricane Agnes in 1972, recognizing the low-market penetration of flood insurance, Congress passed the Flood Disaster Protection Act of 1973[32] to establish a mandatory flood insurance purchase requirement for structures located in identified SFHA. After the 1973 act, federally regulated lenders were obligated to require flood insurance on any loan secured by improved real estate in a FEMA-designated SFHA in a participating community. After the Midwest floods of 1993, it became increasingly apparent to Congress that homeowners were still not adequately complying with the mandatory insurance purchase requirement. The flood provided the impetus for strengthening lender compliance through the mandatory purchase provisions in the 1994 National Flood Insurance Reform Act.[33] Recognition of the impact of properties prone to repetitive flooding on the financial condition of the program led to the passage of the Flood Insurance Reform Act of 2004,[34] which established a pilot program for the mitigation of severe-repetitive-loss properties (SRLPs) and the funding of mitigation activities for individual SRLPs.

After the 2008 and 2011 catastrophic floods, Congress focused attention on long-term reforms and reauthorization of the NFIP to ensure the financial viability of the program, ensure continued comprehensive coverage for all property in floodplains, and explore a private-sector role in financing flood risks. These efforts led to the passage of the Biggert-Waters Flood Insurance Reform Act of 2012.

Identifying and Mapping Areas of Special Flood Risk

Accurate flood maps with the latest engineering and flood modeling digital mapping technologies help to reduce future flood losses and ensure that rates reflect actual risk which, in turn, promotes the fiscal soundness of the NFIP.

---

[31] Dan R. Anderson, "The National Flood Insurance Program: Problem and Potential," *The Journal of Risk and Insurance*, 1974, vol.16 (4), p. 579-599.

[32] P.L. 93-234, 87 Stat. 975.

[33] P.L. 103-325, 108 Stat. 2255.

[34] P.L. 108-264, 118 Stat. 712.

Accuracy of Maps

Flood maps could become outdated and inaccurate when they fail to reflect floodplain and wetland altered by watershed development that destroys the natural system that contains flooding.[35] The altering of rivers and streams by construction of dams, levees, and other flood-control structures arguably increased the risk of inland floods and development throughout the affected floodplains. Similarly, the construction of roads and buildings create impermeable surfaces that reduce the natural environment's ability to absorb or delay water flows and changes in drainage patterns—a situation that could increase flood risk in the affected area. Flood maps might not adequately consider coastal-flood hazards, such as cumulative shoreline erosion or the loss of wetland, which serves as a natural buffer to storm surge and reduces downstream flooding in inland areas.[36]

Basic Mechanics of Flood Mapping

A typical Flood Insurance Study (FIS) begins with modeling of rainfall and storm tide records for the local areas. The data are then simulated to determine the likely discharge that could result from storms of various probabilities. This discharge data is applied to a cross section of the floodplain to estimate flood depths at various locations. Once FEMA determines water surface elevation data in various areas in the community, the next steps are to calculate the depth of flooding for buildings in the area and calculate the dollar damages using a vulnerability function (state-damage curve) derived from past flood events.[37] The Base Flood Elevation (BFE) of the first floor of the structure relative to the flood depth on the floodplain determines property-specific flood risk data to guide construction and insurance decisions. FEMA used this flood hazard data to create FIRMs that delineate areas determined to have a 1% chance of flood in any given year (the "100-year floodplain"). The 1%-annual-chance flood is a flood insurance standard, not a public safety standard.

Flood Risk with Respect to Levees

The Biggert-Waters Flood Insurance Reform Act of 2012 requires FEMA to develop risk models, flood zones, and insurance rates that account for several typical non-accredited levee scenarios. This regulatory reform stems in part from the consequences of the breaching of the levee system protecting the City of New Orleans in 2005 and the massive flood inundation it caused, which led to the most costly flood event in the history of the NFIP. Residents in the SFHA had to purchase flood insurance if they had a federally insured mortgage. FEMA assumed the levee system would prevent the flow of water on the landward side of the levee during the 1%-annual-chance flood event and, therefore, did not adequately price the risk of levee failure or overtopping. FEMA

---

[35] Before FEMA began its map modernization programs, many FIRMs were 20 to 25 years old and did not accurately reflect residual risk behind or below flood control structures, giving residents living behind them a false sense of security.

[36] FEMA designates flood-risk zones on a flood insurance rate according to risk level. The codes are Zones A, AO, A1-A30, AE, AR, AR/AO, AR/A1-A30, AR/AE, AR/AH, AR/A99, A99, AH, VO, V1-V30, VE, and V. These zones are highly susceptible to flooding and, therefore, subject to mandatory flood insurance purchase requirements. V-lettered zones are also subject to wave action. Older maps use Zones B and C to represent areas of moderate- and low-flood risk. Newer maps have replaced these designations with Zone X (shaded) and Zone X (unshaded), respectively.

[37] A *stage-damage curve* is an estimate of damages as a percentage of value based on the depth of flooding experience.

assumes non-accredited levees do not meet the federal standard for reducing the risk associated with a major flood and, therefore, prices this risk.

Funding Flood Hazard Mapping ActivitiesU.S. population.

Table 2 shows recent funding levels for FEMA's flood mapping program. In 2003, FEMA began the Flood Map Modernization (Map Mod) program to update the nation's inventory of FIRMs to digital FIRMs (DFIRMs) for areas of the United States with the greatest flood risk. Map Mod provided updated DFIRMs for more than 92% of the U.S. population.

Table 2. FEMA Flood Mapping Program Funding Levels: FY2011- FY2013

($ in thousands)

Program	FY2011(Enacted)	FY2012 (Enacted)	FY2013 Pres. Budget
Flood Hazard Mapping & Risk Analysis, Risk Map	$204,131	$97,712	$89,329
National Flood Insurance Fund, FIF, Flood Studies & Surveys	$113,509	$117,706	$116,000
Total	**$317,640**	**$215,418**	**$205,329**

Source: U.S. Department of Homeland Security, FEMA's Office of Legislative Affairs.

FEMA's Risk Maps, Assessment, and Planning (Risk MAP) Program

The Map Mod program successfully developed and delivered a new digital platform that has enabled FEMA to make flood hazard data more widely available while providing opportunities to focus on enhancing data accuracy and resolution issues. Other technologies were also developed to provide opportunities to focus efforts on raising risk awareness and building a risk management framework to achieve sustainable actions to reduce and better manage flood risks going forward.

In 2009, FEMA's Map Mod program became the Risk Mapping, Assessment, and Planning (Risk MAP) program that builds on flood hazard data and maps produced during the Map Mod program.[38] Risk MAP is an integrated flood risk management approach that weaves NFIP flood hazard data into watershed-based risk assessments that serve as the basis for local hazard mitigation plans and support community actions to reduce risk.

Under the Risk MAP program, FEMA initiated projects for 37% of the U.S. population through FY2011 and anticipates increasing that number to 43% by the end of FY2012. In addition, FEMA has provided to communities New, Validated or Updated Engineering (NVUE) data for 54% of the miles mapped under the NFIP. By the end of FY2012, FEMA had initiated studies to cover approximately 61% of the miles mapped. FEMA continues to update the nation's coastal-flood hazard studies.

---

[38] See Department of Homeland Security, Federal Emergency Management Agency, "Risk MAP 2010-2014 Multi-Year Plan," at http://www.fema.gov/library/viewRecord.do?id=3587.

Financial Status of NFIP

This section examines the current financial status of NFIP, including borrowing from the U.S. Treasury and remaining financial issues for Congress.

Table 3 shows that the NFIP currently has more than 5.6 million policies in force nationwide covering approximately $1.3 trillion in property in almost 20,000 participating communities. Policyholders paid $3.48 billion in premiums in 2011. The NFIP experienced six catastrophic loss years—defined as payouts of $1 billion or more—in its 44-year history that severely tested the financial resiliency of the program. These years include 1995, 2001, 2004, 2005, 2008, and 2011.

Table 3. NFIP Program Statistics

(as of December 31, 2011; $ nominal)

Calendar Year	Number of Policies in Force	Total Written Premium	Total Face Value of Coverage	Total Number of Claims Paid	Total Payments Made to Policyholders
1972-1977	NA	NA	NA	4,441	$18,035,658
1978	1,446,354	$111,250,585	$50,500,956,000	29,122	$147,719,253
1979	1,843,441	$141,535,832	$74,375,240,000	70,613	$483,281,219
1980	2,103,851	$159,009,583	$99,259,942,000	41,918	$230,414,295
1981	1,915,065	$256,798,488	$102,059,859,000	23,261	$127,118,031
1982	1,900,544	$354,842,356	$107,296,802,000	32,831	$198,295,820
1983	1,981,122	$384,225,425	$117,834,255,000	51,584	$439,454,937
1984	1,926,388	$420,530,032	$124,421,281,000	27,688	$254,642,874
1985	2,016,785	$452,466,332	$139,948,260,000	38,676	$368,238,794
1986	2,119,039	$518,226,957	$155,717,168,000	13,789	$126,384,695
1987	2,115,183	$566,391,536	$165,053,402,000	13,400	$105,432,378
1988	2,149,153	$589,453,163	$175,764,175,000	7,758	$51,022,523
1989	2,292,947	$632,204,396	$265,218,590,000	36,245	$661,658,285
1990	2,477,861	$672,791,834	$213,588,265,000	14,766	$167,896,816
1991	2,532,713	$737,078,033	$223,098,548,000	28,549	$353,681,702
1992	2,623,406	$800,973,357	$236,844,980,000	44,650	$710,225,154
1993	2,828,558	$890,425,274	$267,870,761,000	36,044	$659,059,461
1994	3,040,198	$1,003,850,875	$295,935,328,000	21,583	$411,075,128
1995	3,476,829	$1,140,808,119	$349,137,768,000	62,441	$1,295,578,117
1996	3,693,076	$1,275,176,752	$400,681,650,000	52,677	$828,036,508
1997	4,102,416	$1,509,787,517	$462,606,433,000	30,338	$519,537,378
1998	4,235,138	$1,668,246,681	$497,621,083,000	57,348	$886,327,133
1999	4,329,985	$1,719,652,696	$534,117,781,000	47,247	$754,970,800
2000	4,369,087	$1,723,824,570	$567,568,653,000	16,362	$251,720,536
2001	4,458,470	$1,740,331,079	$611,918,920,000	43,589	$1,277,002,489
2002	4,519,799	$1,802,277,937	$653,776,126,000	25,312	$433,644,094
2003	4,565,491	$1,897,687,479	$691,786,140,000	36,838	$780,492,440
2004	4,667,446	$2,040,828,486	$765,205,681,000	55,825	$2,232,042,331
2005	4,962,011	$2,241,264,140	$876,679,658,000	212,778	$17,713,105,660
2006	5,514,895	$2,604,844,133	$1,054,087,148,000	24,592	$640,623,771
2007	5,655,919	$2,843,422,049	$1,141,242,230,000	23,129	$612,351,594
2008	5,684,275	$3,066,729,200	$1,197,659,846,000	74,266	$3,450,249,017
2009	5,704,198	$3,202,267,224	$1,233,005,263,000	30,821	$772,390,723
2010	5,559,313	$3,348,222,091	$1,227,932,424,400	27,165	$708,992,043
2011	5,585,797	$3,477,338,993	$1,264,043,634,800	65,315	$1,847,881,892

Source: U.S. Department of Homeland Security, FEMA's Office of Legislative Affairs.

Figure 1 shows that over the period from 1978 to 2011, the NFIP experienced nine loss years in which flood loss payments exceeded premiums written.[39] In 2005, Hurricanes Katrina- and Rita-related losses easily dwarf all other loss years. The flood-related losses from the 2005 and 2008 hurricane seasons resulted in substantial NFIP borrowing from the U.S. Treasury that led to the current $17.75 billion in cumulative debt. (See **Table 4**.)

Figure 1. Difference Between Total Premiums Written and Total Payments Made to Policyholders Under the National Flood Insurance Program: 1978-2011

($ nominal)

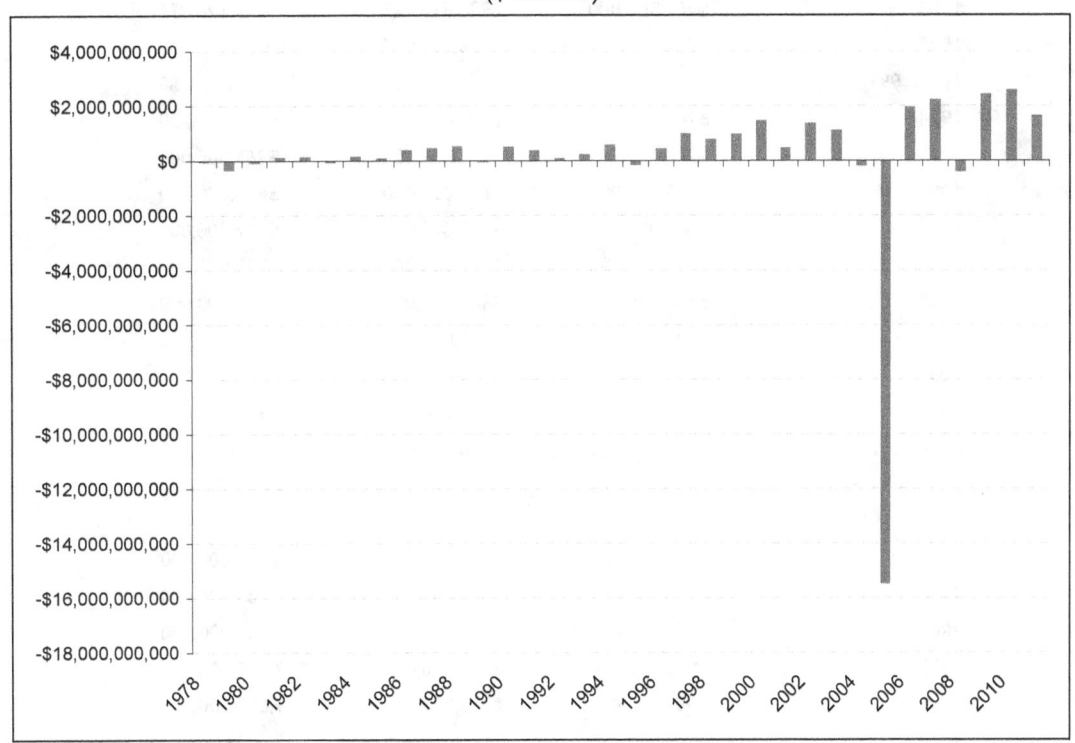

Source: U.S. Department of Homeland Security, Federal Emergency Management Agency.

Treasury Borrowing

Table 4 shows the history of U.S. Treasury borrowing and repayments under the NFIP from 1981 through 2011. The NFIP was self-supporting from 1986 until 2005, covering all administrative expenses and claim payments out of premium income and fees. Since Hurricane Katrina struck in August 2005, FEMA has had to borrow $19.64 billion, which includes $2.6 billion over the 2007-2009 period, to pay claims from Hurricane Ike and the Midwest floods of 2008.[40] The NFIP's borrowing authority was increased to $20.775 billion on March 23, 2006.

---

[39] These unusual flood loss years were 1978, 1979, 1980, 1983, 1989, 1995, 2004, 2005, and 2008.

[40] It appears unlikely that the $17.75 billion in debt to the U.S. Treasury, as of June 30, 2012, will be repaid within the next 10 years given annual interest payments of about $1 billion and annual premium income of approximately $3.5 billion.

Table 4. History of U.S. Treasury Borrowing Under the National Flood Insurance Program

(as of June 30, 2012; $ nominal)

Fiscal Year	Amount Borrowed	Amount Repaid	Cumulative Debt
Prior to 1981[a]	$917,406,008	$0	$917,406,008
1981	$164,614,526	$624,970,099	$457,050,435
1982	$13,915,000	$470,965,435	$0
1983	$50,000,000	$0	$50,000,000
1984[b]	$200,000,000	$36,879,123	$213,120,877
1985	$0	$213,120,877	$0
1986-1993	$0	$0	$0
1994[c]	$100,000,000	$100,000,000	$0
1995	$265,000,000	$0	$265,000,000
1996	$423,600,000	$62,000,000	$626,600,000
1997	$530,000,000	$239,600,000	$917,000,000
1998	$0	$395,000,000	$522,000,000
1999	$400,000,000	$381,000,000	$541,000,000
2000	$345,000,000	$541,000,000	$345,000,000
2001	$600,000,000	$345,000,000	$600,000,000
2002	$50,000,000	$640,000,000	$10,000,000
October 2002	$0	$10,000,000	$0
2003 (Nov-Sep)	$0	$0	$0
2004	$0	$0	$0
2005[d]	$300,000,000	$75,000,000	$225,000,000
2006	$16,660,000,000	$0	$16,885,000,000
2007	$650,000,000	$0	$17,535,000,000
2008	$50,000,000	$225,000,000	$17,360,000,000
2009	$1,987,988,421	$347,988,421	$19,000,000,000
2010	$0	$500,000,000	$18,500,000,000
2011	$0	$750,000,000	$17,750,000,000
Total	**$23,707,523,955**	**$5,957,523,955**	**$17,750,000,000**

Source: U.S. Department of Homeland Security, Federal Emergency Management Agency's Office of Legislative Affairs.

Notes: Borrowings through 1985 were repaid from congressional appropriations. The NFIP did not borrow from 1986 through 1993. Since 1994, borrowings are repaid from premium and other income. The existing debt outstanding is expected to be repaid with premium income or with congressional appropriations.

a. Balance forward from U.S. Department of Housing and Urban Development.

b. Figure for the $213.1 million in cumulative debt in 1984 provided by FEMA reflects additional cost outside of the insurance program.

c. Of the $100 million borrowed, only $11 million was needed to cover obligations.

d. NFIP borrowed $300 million in 2005 to pay claims from the 2004 hurricane season, but Hurricanes Katrina, Rita, and Wilma struck after late August 2005, and claims were submitted after the 2006 fiscal year began.

The Biggert-Waters Flood Insurance Reform Act of 2012 (referred to hereafter as the 2012 Reform Act) requires FEMA to establish a reserve fund to offset claims during catastrophic loss years to reduce the likelihood of the NFIP having to borrow from the Treasury.[41] Although the 2012 Reform Act does not forgive any portion of the NFIP debt, it requires FEMA to create a repayment schedule for funds borrowed from the Treasury and directs FEMA to include catastrophic loss years when assessing flood risk in order to set annual premium rates.[42] The latter requirement allows the program to collect risk-based premiums that, in theory, would reduce the likelihood of the program encountering financial deficits that result in program borrowing from the Treasury. Some experts believe that even if FEMA increased flood insurance rates up to the maximum amount allowed under the new law (20% per year), the program would still not have sufficient funds to cover future obligations for policyholder claims, operating expenses, and interest on debt.

Factors Affecting Financial Soundness of the NFIP

In considering the NFIP's financial solvency, it may be useful to recognize two things: (1) the NFIP was not capitalized at inception by Congress and (2) the program does not operate under the traditional insurance definition of fiscal solvency that requires the insurer to have statutory reserves as a condition of receiving authorization to sell insurance in a given state.

Premium Subsidies

Before the passage of the Flood Reform Act of 2012, the NFIP faced a long-term solvency challenge because the program did not have a financing mechanism for handling catastrophic losses and it charged less-than-actuarial rates for pre-FIRM structures.[43] Annual premiums were not likely to cover the program's long-term expenses, claim costs, and interest and principal debt repayment to the U.S. Treasury. Therefore, taxpayers faced financial exposure from recurring catastrophic flood events.[44] FEMA's old rate-setting structure was designed to generate premiums at least sufficient to cover losses and loss adjustment expenses relative to the "historical average loss year."[45] There was no contingent amount added to premiums to build a surplus. When losses and expenses exceeded premiums, the program was authorized to borrow from the U.S. Treasury but had to repay the funds with interest.

---

[41] P.L. 112-141; 126 Stat. 916, Section 100212.

[42] Ibid, Section 100211.

[43] Buildings constructed after December 31, 1974, or after the publication of a flood insurance rate map (FIRM), are charged an actuarial premium that reflects the property's risk of flooding. Subsidized rates, on the other hand, are determined by a statutory mandate that requires rates to be affordable so individuals are encouraged to participate. Owners of properties built prior to the issuance of a community's flood hazard map or January 1, 1974 (Pre-Firm structures), usually pay subsidized rates and are exempted from the NFIP's floodplain management standards. Even properties that are remapped into higher-risk areas pay the subsidized rates—a situation that exacerbates the financial challenges facing the NFIP.

[44] U.S. Government Accountability Office, FEMA's Rate-Setting Process Warrants Attention," GAO-09-12, October 31, 2008.

[45] In contrast, commercial insurance premiums are typically set at a level that covers expected losses and expenses plus an amount for a profit margin. A portion of each premium dollar collected is then set aside in loss reserves, which are invested and used to pay claims and expenses.

Many experts insisted that the NFIP would not be financially sound until actuarial risk-based rates were charged. FEMA reports that 78% of policyholders already pay actuarial premiums, albeit there is some debate about whether rates reflect the true flood risk to people and property.[46] Charging rates that fully reflect flood risk arguably would discourage development in the most risky areas.

The new law eliminated subsidized premium rates and allowed rates to be adjusted to reflect true risk, taking into consideration historical loss data, including catastrophic loss years and other factors, such as coastal storm surge and climate change.[47] To address the affordability issue, the new law authorized a study of the feasibility of an insurance voucher system or similar means tested assistance.[48] As indicate earlier, the Flood Reform Act of 2012 established a catastrophe fund to stabilize catastrophe losses from year to year.[49]

Repetitive Flood Loss Properties

Properties that experience repetitive flood losses, known as a "repetitive loss properties" (RLP) and "severe repetitive loss properties" (SRLP), account for a disproportionately large share of all the flood insurance claims filed and paid under the NFIP.[50] Historically, it is estimated that approximately 1% of the properties insured under the NFIP have accounted for over a third of claims paid. About 1 in 10 homes that suffer repetitive flood damages have cumulative flood insurance claims that have exceeded the value of the house.[51] FEMA estimates that 90% of all RLPs were built prior to December 31, 1974, or before the adoption of a FIRM—and, hence, have been subject to premium discounts. Importantly, the annual increase in new RLPs is outpacing FEMA mitigation efforts by a factor of 10 to 1. After the 1993 Midwest flood, FEMA and other federal government agencies spent hundreds of millions of dollars to remove frequently flooded properties from the floodplain.

Table 5 shows that since 1978, a total of 166,368 RLPs have had 496,178 claims paid, which has cost the National Flood Insurance Fund a total of $12.1 billion in nominal dollars. **Appendix A** shows RLPs by state. The average claim for these properties was $24,388.

---

[46] Federal Emergency Management Agency, "Actuarial Rate Review: In Support of the October 1, 2010, Rate and Rule Changes," July 2010, p. 22.

[47] P.L. 112-141; 126 Stat. 916, Section 100211.

[48] Ibid., Section 100236.

[49] Ibid., Section 100212.

[50] A repetitive loss property (RLP) is defined as an insured property that experiences two or more flood losses greater than $1,000 within any 10-year period. A subset of RLPs, called severe repetitive loss properties (SRLP), have incurred at least four NFIP claim payments of at least $5,000 each or the cumulative amount of such claims payments exceeds $20,000 or for which at least two separate claims have been made with the cumulative amount of the building portion of such claims exceeding the market value of the building.

[51] U.S. Department of Homeland Security, Office of Inspector General, *FEMA's Implementation of the Flood Insurance Reform Act of 2004*, OIG-09-45, March 26, 2009, p. 4, at http://www.dhs.gov/xoig/assets/mgmtrpts/OIG_09-45_Mar09.pdf.

Table 5. Total Repetitive Flood Loss Properties in the NFIP: 1978-2011

(as of December 31, 2011: $ nominal)

Building Payments	$9,332,087,006
Contents Payments	$2,768,293,788
Total payments	$12,100,980,774
Average payment	$24,388
Number of Losses	496,178
Number of Properties	166,368

Source: U.S. Department of Homeland Security, Federal Emergency Management Agency.

FEMA has undertaken several actions over the years to address the RLP problem. The initial strategy, announced in 1999, was to identify the nation's inventory of RLPs and focus on structures that were substantially damaged (i.e., damaged 50% or more of market value) at which time they would be reconstructed, elevated, or flood-proofed to prevent future damage. One reported difficulty has been reluctance and inconsistency at the local community level in declaring structures substantially damaged, which triggers the requirement to rebuild to a higher flood construction standard.

FEMA also pursued a strategy of phasing out premium subsidies on RLPs through voluntary buyouts or the imposition of full actuarially based rates on RLP owners who refuse to accept FEMA's offer to mitigate the effect of flood damage. In addition, the agency incorporated special incentives into the Community Rating System and provided data to states and communities to help them address the RLPs.

The Flood Insurance Reform Act of 2004[52] required FEMA to establish the Repetitive Flood Claims (RFC) and the Severe Repetitive Loss (SRL) Grant programs to provide funding to reduce or eliminate the long-term risk of flood damage under the NFIP. The RFC program offers grants to states and local governments to mitigate future flood losses. Mitigation projects typically include demolishing, relocating, elevating, or flood-proofing structures. However, the SRL program has proven to be cumbersome for communities and states to administer. Currently, there are more than 12,300 SRL policies being serviced in the NFIP-Special Direct Facility (NFIP-SDF).

The Biggert-Waters Flood Insurance Reform Act of 2012 streamlined and reauthorized the Flood Mitigation Assistance Program (FMA), the RFC, and the SRL to allow federal funds to be used for mitigation of repetitive- or severe-repetitive-loss structures to improve their effectiveness and efficiency.[53]

Low NFIP Program Participation

The intent and success of the NFIP rests on making affordable flood insurance widely available to the general public and protecting communities from potential damage through floodplain management. Since 1973, federal regulations have required flood insurance on structures located

---

[52] P.L. 108-264; 118 Stat. 712.

[53] P.L. 112-141, Section 100225.

in identified Special Flood Hazard Areas (SFHAs) that have a federally backed mortgage. Also, since 1994, recipients of certain flood disaster assistance have been required to purchase and hold flood insurance to protect against future flood losses, under penalty of receiving no federal disaster aid in subsequent floods.[54] Despite the existence of this mandatory flood insurance purchase requirement, take-up rates for flood insurance have historically been low and the federal government's exposure to uninsured property losses from flooding remains substantial. Many homeowners do not completely recognize or internalize their flood risk and are overly optimistic about the magnitude of the flood risk to which they are exposed. Consequently, the NFIP has not achieved the level of individual participation originally envisioned by Congress.

Researchers indicate that there are at least five possible explanations for the low market penetration for flood insurance: (1) flood insurance is not seen as being worth the cost (i.e., a poor investment); (2) individuals have misperceptions about low-probability risks and lack information about the NFIP;[55] (3) private insurance agents do not market NFIP policies; (4) lack of compliance with the mandatory purchase requirement or failure to ensure that property owners maintain coverage for the life of the loan; and (5) many homeowners in risky areas either do not have a mortgage or have a mortgage from a lender that does not enforce the mandatory purchase requirement.

A study of the NFIP's mandatory purchase requirement nationwide conducted by the Rand Corporation indicated that only about 49% of single-family homes in SFHAs are covered by flood insurance.[56] In the absence of flood insurance, the cost of repairing flood-damaged property is usually borne by either the property owner from their own financial resources or with assistance through federal relief programs, instead of by flood insurance payments. This situation has resulted in billions of dollars of uninsured property losses and arguably results in higher social costs.

FEMA lacks nationwide data on the number of properties in floodplains that makes it difficult to accurately determine insurance market penetration. Available evidence suggests that penetration rates in the 100-year floodplain are consistently low. A 2006 Rand Corporation study estimated that about 49% of properties in SFHAs purchased NFIP flood insurance.[57] Concerns have also been expressed about the large number of homes that are not mortgaged and thus are not required to be insured against flood risks.

The Biggert-Waters Flood Insurance Reform Act of 2012 addressed the lack of enforcement of the mandatory insurance purchase requirement by increasing the amount of civil penalties that can be imposed against regulated lending institutions that fail to require flood insurance from $350 to $2,000 per violation.[58]

---

[54] CRS Report RS22945, *Flood Insurance Requirements for Stafford Act Assistance*, by Edward C. Liu.

[55] Howard C. Kunreuther, "The Changing Societal Consequences of Risks from Natural Hazards." *Annals of the American Academy of Political and Social Science* 1979, vol. 443, pp. 104-116.

[56] Rand Institute for Civil Justice, "The National Flood Insurance Program's Market Penetration Rate: Estimates and Policy Implications," available at http://www.rand.org/pubs/technical_reports/2006/RAND_TR300.pdf.

[57] Rand Institute for Civil Justice, "The National Flood Insurance Program's Market Penetration Rate: Estimates and Policy Implications," at http://www.rand.org/pubs/technical_reports/2006/RAND_TR300.pdf.

[58] P.L. 112-141; Section 100208.

Inaccurate Flood Hazard Maps

FEMA is responsible for identifying and mapping the nation's floodplain areas and identifying flood-risk zones in such areas. Flood Insurance Rate Maps (FIRMs) are used for setting flood insurance rates, regulating floodplain development, and communicating information about the 1%-annual-chance flood hazard to those who live in floodplains. FIRMs also are used to determine whether property owners are required by law to obtain flood insurance as a condition of obtaining mortgage loans or other federally related financial assistance. Without accurate and updated flood hazard maps, property owners and small businesses could underestimate their exposure to flood risks and make poor financial decisions about protecting their properties (i.e., where to build and whether to purchase flood insurance or take other measures to protect their properties).

The Biggert-Waters Flood Insurance Reform Act of 2012 authorized several regulatory changes to improve the accuracy of flood maps and established a process to allow communities to request a remapping based on the standards recommended by a newly established Technical Mapping Advisory Council and adopted by FEMA.[59] The new law also authorized the creation of an independent Scientific Resolution Panel consisting of experts on flood hazard maps and flood insurance to address mapping-related concerns from communities that are dissatisfied with the outcome of their appeal to FEMA.[60]

Lack of Enforcement of Floodplain Management Regulations

The Biggert-Waters Flood Insurance Reform Act of 2012 requires FEMA to conduct a study of the impact, effectiveness, and feasibility of including widely used and nationally recognized building codes as part of the floodplain management criteria. The new law would also allow the use of funds under the Community Development Block Grant Program (CDBG) to include community building code administration grants.[61]

Under the NFIP, FEMA is prohibited from providing flood insurance to property owners residing in communities not participating in the NFIP.[62] Local communities must adopt and enforce certain minimum floodplain management ordinances as a condition for participation in the NFIP. However, efforts to guide construction and development away from high-risk areas through community-based land-use and zoning ordinances have reportedly been subordinated to building and elevation requirements that lead to further development of the floodplains.[63] Even in hazard-prone floodways and coastal areas, building and rebuilding are allowed under NFIP standards, with the cost of insurance varying with property elevation.

---

[59] Ibid, Section 100216.

[60] Ibid, Section 100218.

[61] Ibid. Section 100243.

[62] 44 CFR 59.21.

[63] National Wildlife Federation, *Heavy Rainfall and Increased Flooding Risk: Global Warming's Wake-up Call for the Central United States*, 2008, at http://www.nwf.org/extremeweather/pdfs/Heavy_Rainfall_and_Increased_Flooding-Wake-Up_Call_for_Central_U.S2.pdf.

Coastal Flood Hazard Risk Assessment and Mapping

One issue of contention that emerged from the controversy and litigation surrounding Katrina-related wind versus water insurance claims disputes was whether the NFIP should be expanded to allow policyholders to purchase optional wind coverage. Following the storm, individuals and businesses in Louisiana, Mississippi, and Alabama protested against what they claimed were inappropriate obstacles to the payment of their property damage insurance claims. When insurance adjustors and damage experts assessed the properties damaged by Hurricane Katrina, they were faced with the issue of allocating damages between wind (a covered loss) and flood (an excluded loss). Post-Katrina insurance claims litigation and the delays and economic uncertainty generated for consumers and insurers raised concerns about post-event judicial interpretations of the scope of insurance coverage.

Proponents of optional wind coverage under the NFIP argued that this policy change was necessary because of the difficulties property owners faced in obtaining affordable private wind coverage in states along the Gulf and Atlantic Coasts. Private insurers had increased premiums and deductibles and reduced coverage or withdrawn altogether from these areas out of concern about catastrophic risk exposure.

Opponents of adding wind coverage to the NFIP believed there was adequate wind coverage capacity in every state through either the traditional private market or through the state residual market program (e.g., wind pools). Critics maintained that expanding the NFIP to add wind coverage would dramatically increase the financial exposure of the NFIP and, hence, federal taxpayers. Concerns were also expressed about the NFIP's ability to determine actuarially sound rates for the windstorm portion of this coverage and avoid wide-scale financial deficits in the program following a catastrophic flood event.

Moreover, there were concerns that even actuarial rates may not produce sufficient premium income to cover the program's administration costs and losses in the event of a catastrophic event. The Government Accountability Office (GAO) issued a report in 2008 that outlined some difficulties that FEMA could face in implementing an optional wind coverage provision. Some of the obstacles included (1) the concern about "adverse selection" or the likelihood that only those property owners at highest risk would purchase coverage; (2) wind hazard prevention standards that communities would have to adopt to receive coverage; (3) uncertainty about the adoption of programs to accommodate wind coverage; (4) difficulties in establishing a new rate-setting process; (5) enforcement of new building codes; and (6) administration and oversight of the program.[64]

The Biggert-Waters Flood Insurance Reform Act of 2012 established the COASTAL program to authorize the use of scientific coastal hazard data collected by NOAA in conjunction with engineering formulas to be developed by FEMA to accurately assess flood insurance claims for total-loss, "slab" properties.[65] The aim of the COASTAL program is to better estimate wind versus water risks and allocate insured losses following a major hurricane, storm surge, or tornado.

---

[64] U.S. Government Accountability Office, GAO-08-504, *National Catastrophe Insurance: Analysis of Proposed Combined Federal Flood and Wind Insurance Program*, April 25, 2008.

[65] P.L. 112-141; Section 100252.

Moral Hazard and Federal Disaster Assistance

According to the written testimony of Administrator Craig Fugate of FEMA, most owners of flood-prone property in NFIP-participating communities opted to not purchase flood insurance prior to a purchase mandate, choosing instead to rely on federal disaster assistance to finance their recovery.[66] As discussed above, the low-penetration rate of NFIP continues and suggests that many people may still rely on federal disaster assistance instead of flood insurance. In economic theory, the assurance of federal assistance in the event of repeated disaster-related losses may create a "moral hazard" by lowering the incentives to take appropriate steps to mitigate loss. This situation counteracts one of the original objectives of the NFIP, which is to develop mitigation plans and implement measures (insurance linked to land management) to reduce future flood damages and the cost of taxpayer-funded disaster assistance.

In 1977, President Jimmy Carter signed into law Executive Order 11988 to require federal agencies to avoid direct and indirect support of floodplain development in coastal velocity zones —the so-called V zones on FIRMs —by taking action "to reduce the risk of flood loss, to minimize the impact of floods on human safety, health and welfare, and to restore and preserve the natural and beneficial values served by floodplains in carrying out its responsibilities."[67] Under E.O. 11988, FEMA staff must (1) determine eligibility and the required elevation of all new construction in coastal high-hazard areas on the Gulf Coast and (2) decide whether new structures, the costs of repair, or the replacement of facilities in V zones are eligible for FEMA funding.

Although regulatory guidelines for E.O. 11988 are outlined in 44 CFR Part 9, there has arguably been a lack of clarity in interpreting those guidelines to determine whether officials are to support recovery and community development in V zones. Access to federal assistance for recovery and hazard mitigation projects undertaken in V zones could emerge as an important issue in the aftermath of Hurricane Sandy. The decision to approve and obligate FEMA recovery funds for public assistance projects located in V zones could be an essential consideration in the reconstruction or redevelopment of some coastal areas devastated by Hurricane Sandy.

Remaining Issues for Possible Congressional Oversight

Since 2008, when the NFIP lost its authorization, Congress has passed 17 short-term extensions and the program has lapsed four times (See **Appendix C**). The Biggert-Waters Flood Insurance Reform Act of 2012 did not resolve all flood management issues pertaining to the NFIP. The new law reflects a consensus as of that moment in time with respect to the financial stability and administrative efficiency of the NFIP, the need to have those who reside in flood-prone areas to pay for that risk, and the need for strengthening the mapping program. However, several policy

---

[66] Testimony of Craig Fugate, administrator of Federal Emergency Management Agency, before the Senate Committee on Banking, Housing, and Urban Affairs, *National Flood Insurance Program Reform*, June 9, 2011, p. 3, located at http://banking.senate.gov/public/index.cfm?FuseAction=Files.View&FileStore_id=c6f08bf5-5daa-4406-b461-1781159ec9c1.

[67] U.S. President Jimmy Carter, "Floodplain Management" Executive Order 11988, *Federal Register*, May 24, 1977, p. 26951, at http://www.fema.gov/plan/ehp/ehplaws/attachments-laws/eo11988.pdf.

---

issues and questions remain for future congressional consideration. These remaining issues and questions include the following:

The nation's increasing flood risk vulnerability in an era of frequent extreme weather and climatic events and population growth in flood-prone areas

- What are the true costs borne by the federal government under the NFIP with consideration of both the direct effects and indirect social and economic costs?

- What additional steps, if any, should the federal government undertake to effectively manage and mitigate flood disasters and discourage overdevelopment in flood vulnerable areas?

- How best to strengthen coordination among the nation's water resources and floodplain management agencies at the federal, state, and local levels of government?

- Is there a need to plan for the sustainability of the NFIP in an environment of increasingly frequent catastrophic flooding across the country?

Affordability of insurance coverage in era of actuarial (full-risk) premium pricing

- Is coverage of the NFIP wide enough?

- Will the changes made under the Biggert-Waters Flood Insurance Reform Act of 2012 be adequate to address this concern?

- What is the feasibility of vouchers for low-income NFIP policyholders who are not able to pay actuarial flood insurance rates?

- What is the best approach to balance the government's need to increase the NFIP's future income versus making the insurance coverage affordable and widely available?

- Would the privatization of flood risk make insurance more affordable or less so? Is the private sector up to the task? Is there capacity to underwrite this risk?

Debt forgiveness

- Should Congress eliminate the NFIP's debt to the Treasury?

- What are the distributional consequences across different stakeholders of debt forgiveness?

- Will the NFIP reserve fund be sufficient to offset future catastrophic loss years?

Accuracy of flood hazard maps and risk assessment methods

- The goal of flood mapping is to identify areas that periodically flood. Is there still a need for accurate, up-dated flood maps linked to new risk assessment methodologies applicable to coastal hazards and residual risk behind levees?

- Is there a need for consistency between U.S. Army Corps of Engineers and FEMA levee certification, that is, a definition of flood protection? What is the best way to improve risk communication with respect to flood control structures?

- What will be the effectiveness of FEMA's efforts to have the level of risk reflected in flood insurance rates?

Movement toward a comprehensive integrated watershed management framework of risk perception, risk management, and disaster response strategy

- Is it time for a holistic comprehensive water resources and mitigation planning process that encourages flood and water resources planning and flood mitigation on a watershed basis? How best to promote a comprehensive approach to resource management on a watershed basis?

- What is the best approach to strengthening local floodplain management and planning and guide development and building practices in regulated floodplains to save lives and reduce property damage?

Feasibility of catastrophic disaster insurance

- What is the best approach to address misperceptions about the nature of the NFIP and barriers to public understanding of flooding and flood risk?

- Should the NFIP cover all claims associated with catastrophic losses or just claims in the average annual loss year?

Coastal hazards risk assessment

- What is the feasibility of NOAA and FEMA developing accurate and consistent coastal hazard risk assessment and mapping tools and methodologies?

- What would it take to produce both flood risk and coastal hazard vulnerability maps?

Federal disaster assistance and moral hazard

- Does the presence of federal disaster assistance introduce moral hazard in flood management in a way that inappropriately shifts risk to taxpayers?[68] Property owners may choose not to purchase the coverage, relying instead on federal disaster assistance to finance recovery. Is there a need to better coordinate the need for insurance coverage rather than access to government relief for post-flood recovery? Separately, some experts have suggested that access to federal disaster assistance under the Stafford Act could have the unintended consequence of shielding communities from the full implications of their decisions on land use

---

[68] Government disaster assistance is usually available only for uninsurable damages. The recipients of disaster assistance do not bear direct cost for remittances. However, the availability of disaster assistance could produce a moral hazard problem. It could reinforce vulnerabilities and provide little incentive to reduce risky behavior. Moreover, disaster assistance could reduce the direct costs associated with risky behavior, where costs are shifted to taxpayers.

and families from the financial consequences of rebuilding in disaster-prone areas.

Options for Managing and Financing Flood Risk

Despite billions invested in flood management, the United States has not been able to curb the rising costs of flood damage and public and private development in flood risk areas. This was the conclusion of the Gilbert F. White National Flood Policy Forum held in November 2007 at George Washington University.[69] The forum brought together 92 diverse experts to consider the future of floodplain management under a "business-as-usual scenario" and under an alternative scenario of aggressive action to address increasing flood risk in the nation. The experts at the forum concluded that an unprecedented set of conditions (e.g., population growth and migration, changes in climate, and degradation of water-based resources) now faces the United States that could increase flood losses more rapidly in the future. Several policy options emerged, and are listed below.

Long-Term Flood Insurance Contracts

Long-term flood insurance contracts (LTFIC) coupled with mitigation loans arguably would encourage investment in risk-reduction measures.70 The idea is for private insurers to offer 5-, 10-, or 20-year flood insurance contracts combined with long-term mitigation loans (e.g., for retrofitting, elevation, and flood-proofing of structures) tied to the mortgage. Mitigation loans would be offered to help finance the high upfront costs associated with investing in mitigation measures. The long-term flood insurance policies would have a maturity that corresponds to the length of the mortgage on the property and the policy would not terminate when the property owner sells the property.

The economic rationale for using LTFI to pre-fund disaster costs is that insurers, generally, need guaranteed premiums for a long time period if rates are to be based on expected losses. By lengthening the term of the property insurance contract, and spreading the risk through a mandatory purchase requirement, LTFI contracts could implicitly permit insurers to compensate for their present inability to prepare adequately for rare and unpredictable flood events.

Privatization of Flood Risk

FEMA has a responsibility to examine the NFIP's contingent liabilities and recommend ways to provide financial stability to the federal flood insurance program. This activity is performed in conjunction with the program's annual rate-setting process. In 2000, FEMA undertook a study with the assistance of accounting firm Deloitte & Touche to explore alternative financing arrangements to reduce the need for U.S. Treasury borrowing.[71] FEMA was concerned about the

---

[69] Association of State Flood Plain managers, *Floodplain Management 2050: A Report of the 2007 Assembly of the Gilbert F. White National Flood Policy Forum*, November 6-7, 2007.

[70] For more information see Carolyn Kouky and Howard Kunreuther, "Improving Flood Insurance and Flood Risk Management: Insights from St. Louis, Missouri," *Resources for the Future*, February 2009, at http://www.rff.org/rff/documents/rff-dp-09-07.pdf.

[71] Federal Emergency Management Agency, *National Flood Insurance Program: Discussion of Financial Stabilization* (continued...)

NFIP's erratic cash flow and the potential for catastrophic losses within a short period of time. One option that received considerable attention was to create a reinsurance vehicle to finance catastrophic losses. After review by the Office of Management and Budget (OMB), this option was not adopted because it was determined that the cost to borrow from the U.S. Treasury was lower.

Recognizing the shortcomings of the current financing arrangement under the NFIP, two basic alternatives have emerged: an all-hazard insurance approach and a federal-insurance (reinsurance) framework that would enable private insurers to cover more flood risks. With the development of computer simulation catastrophe risk models and remote sensing technologies, some private insurers have argued that flood hazards are now insurable by private companies working in partnership with government. Some economists have suggested that floods and other catastrophic risks are now insurable because of insurers' ability to transfer catastrophic risks to the capital markets through securitization of the risk. In this context, FEMA could require private insurers to "make available" private flood insurance policies at actuarially determined prices in flood-prone areas with the federal government providing federal reinsurance. Professors Dwight Jaffee, at University of California, Berkley, and Howard Kunreuther, at the Wharton School, the University of Pennsylvania, are leading proponents for the long-term flood insurance contract proposal.[72]

The Biggert-Waters Flood Insurance Reform Act of 2012 requires FEMA and GAO to study the option of privatizing the program and to report to Congress within one year of enactment.[73] The new law also mandated the director of the Federal Insurance Office to study the current state of the market for natural disaster insurance in the United States.[74]

Community-Based Flood Insurance Policy Contracts

The local community purchases a group policy from the NFIP on behalf of residents in a designated SFHA. Policies are issued to all residents and are paid either through property taxes or as a utility payment. On September 10, 2012, the House of Representatives passed H.R. 6186 to require FEMA to undertake a study of the feasibility of voluntary community-based flood insurance options and how such options could be incorporated into the NFIP. The bill requires the GAO to review and provide an analysis of the FEMA study and to report its findings and recommendations to Congress within one year.

Conclusion

The current system of managing and financing flood risk (NFIP) is about $18 billion in debt. On July 6, 2012, President Obama signed into law H.R. 4348 that included the Biggert-Waters Flood Insurance Reform Act of 2012. This new law made broad changes to the NFIP, ranging from implementing a four-year phase out of premium rate subsidies that have undermined the financial

---

(...continued)

Possibilities, FEMA Unpublished Internal Document, November 20, 2000.

[72] Dwight Jaffee, Howard Kunreuther, and Erwann Michel-Kerjan, *Long Term Insurance (LTI) for Addressing Catastrophic Risk*, National Bureau of Economic Research, Working Paper 14210, August 2008.

[73] P.L. 112-141; Sect.100232.

[74] Ibid., Sec. 100247.

viability of the program, ensuring that maps are updated and accurate and take into account anticipated sea-level rise and residual risk behind levees so that people understand and can better prepare for their risks, encouraging broad participation in the NFIP, streamlining and strengthening mitigation programs to help decrease flood risk, and protecting flood-exposed homes, businesses, and communities better.

Some nevertheless question whether the NFIP still provides appropriate protection against the peril of flood losses and helps build resilient communities. The success of the NFIP will be judged in part by how it handles four major challenges.

The accuracy and reliability of FEMA's flood mapping process. FEMA's Risk Mapping, Assessment, and Planning (Risk MAP) provides quality flood hazard data and tools to increase public awareness and help people make better decisions to protect themselves and communities to enforce floodplain management regulations that support the building of sustainable and resilient communities.[75]

The financial soundness of the NFIP requires flood insurance premiums to fully reflect a building's actuarial risk. Requiring property owners to pay full-actuarial rates that reflect actual risk makes perfect economic sense but it could make flood policies less unaffordable and, therefore, not marketable.

The existing regulatory framework for residual flood risk behind certified 100-year levees has created a perceived safety that spurs development behind the levee systems.[76] Individuals might think a flood occurring once in a 100-year period could not harm them and, therefore, choose not to financial protection against this risk. Most disaster experts would agree that resolution of the nation's flood management challenge must involve hazard-mitigation measures that get people and communities to retreat or avoid living in flood-prone areas while supporting the building of hazard-resilient coastal communities that have the ability to recover quickly and learn from negative experiences.

There is the perception of the inequitable distribution of the NFIP's costs and benefits across income groups and geographic regions.

---

[75] See Department of Homeland Security, Federal Emergency Management Agency, "FEMA's Risk Mapping, Assessment, and Planning (Risk MAP), Fiscal Year 2012 Report To Congress," February 23, 2012, at http://www.fema.gov/library/viewRecord.do?id=5924.

[76] Under 44 CFR 65.10 regulations, FEMA removes areas protected from certified 100-year levees from the flood map. Individuals are then not required to purchase flood insurance and floodplain management standards are not applicable in these areas. If a levee is not certified, FEMA will designate the area behind the levee as a risk and the mandatory purchase requirement will apply.

Appendix A. National Flood Insurance Program's Repetitive Flood Loss Properties

Table A-1. Repetitive Flood Loss Properties in the National Flood Insurance Program

(as of December 31, 2011; $ nominal)

State Name	Building Payments	Contents Payments	Total Payments	Average Payment	Losses	Properties
Alabama	$402,612,962.16	$81,730,441.39	$484,343,403.55	$35,084.64	13,805	4,833
Alaska	$972,686.23	$137,448.10	$1,110,134.33	$13,375.11	83	31
Arizona	$7,732,063.08	$1,372,949.13	$9,105,012.21	$15,251.28	597	258
Arkansas	$37,637,695.99	$9,726,561.34	$47,364,257.33	$21,249.11	2,229	808
California	$155,312,672.34	$37,638,334.53	$192,951,006.87	$21,175.48	9,112	3,299
Colorado	$1,010,193.40	$354,498.51	$1,364,691.91	$10,338.58	132	57
Connecticut	$72,987,538.72	$21,270,677.91	$94,258,216.63	$18,053.67	5,221	1,667
Delaware	$24,442,431.44	$13,222,588.18	$37,665,019.62	$34,778.41	1,083	395
District Columbia	$613,444.22	$16,919.85	$630,364.07	$19,101.94	33	14
Florida	$1,074,522,754.69	$283,995,996.57	$1,358,518,751.26	$32,274.99	42,092	16,546
Georgia	$103,724,414.09	$26,811,644.87	$130,536,058.96	$29,768.77	4,385	1,604
Guam	$363,009.86	$52,467.45	$415,477.31	$13,849.24	30	14
Hawaii	$10,801,779.20	$2,274,003.49	$13,075,782.69	$24,953.78	524	187
Idaho	$591,608.96	$100,132.05	$691,741.01	$10,980.02	63	24
Illinois	$124,766,766.99	$27,723,077.14	$152,489,844.13	$12,761.72	11,949	3,954
Indiana	$54,697,450.19	$10,569,246.21	$65,266,696.40	$16,143.14	4,043	1,467
Iowa	$52,098,900.80	$12,491,664.61	$64,590,565.41	$23,694.26	2,726	1,033
Kansas	$21,231,625.75	$9,189,450.32	$30,421,076.07	$24,278.59	1,253	445
Kentucky	$89,312,937.78	$28,477,331.70	$117,790,269.48	$19,459.82	6,053	1,817
Louisiana	$2,029,521,249.82	$646,722,728.26	$2,676,243,978.08	$27,472.04	97,417	29,472
Maine	$10,313,173.36	$2,844,104.99	$13,157,278.35	$20,917.77	629	235
Maryland	$43,185,640.35	$15,594,237.25	$58,779,877.60	$25,259.94	2,327	959
Massachusetts	$131,940,529.86	$28,353,371.58	$160,293,901.44	$17,776.86	9,017	3,045
Michigan	$13,402,503.32	$5,179,082.14	$18,581,585.46	$10,975.54	1,693	655
Minnesota	$22,679,730.39	$3,707,955.03	$26,387,685.42	$16,298.76	1,619	644
Mississippi	$456,372,579.11	$132,138,941.21	$588,511,520.32	$33,232.34	17,709	6,139
Missouri	$224,032,976.31	$98,902,428.05	$322,935,404.36	$18,040.08	17,901	5,124
Montana	$1,899,435.24	$225,584.67	$2,125,019.91	$13,889.02	153	68
Nebraska	$9,232,709.39	$3,031,207.41	$12,263,916.80	$12,909.39	950	380
Nevada	$6,955,148.57	$3,435,927.12	$10,391,075.69	$59,377.58	175	76

State Name	Building Payments	Contents Payments	Total Payments	Average Payment	Losses	Properties
New Hampshire	$17,452,959.68	$2,677,136.28	$20,130,095.96	$23,111.48	871	338
New Jersey	$715,423,006.56	$209,398,401.52	$924,821,408.08	$21,836.03	42,353	12,432
New Mexico	$1,187,339.29	$60,885.43	$1,248,224.72	$13,716.76	91	39
New York	$385,475,945.74	$104,436,883.54	$489,912,829.28	$16,433.96	29,811	10,712
North Carolina	$404,534,147.25	$69,935,397.40	$474,469,544.65	$19,658.17	24,136	8,664
North Dakota	$23,279,423.10	$2,517,270.79	$25,796,693.89	$29,448.28	876	379
Ohio	$91,459,636.06	$29,487,550.73	$120,947,186.79	$19,237.66	6,287	2,268
Oklahoma	$45,972,663.99	$14,183,242.06	$60,155,906.05	$19,405.13	3,100	958
Oregon	$17,795,025.67	$5,818,442.24	$23,613,467.91	$26,237.19	900	339
Pennsylvania	$446,636,272.49	$127,959,807.52	$574,596,080.01	$25,615.02	22,432	7,878
Puerto Rico	$17,228,403.79	$39,202,639.67	$56,431,043.46	$9,027.52	6,251	2,040
Rhode Island	$26,195,718.48	$13,469,137.25	$39,664,855.73	$35,798.61	1,108	396
South Carolina	$70,906,728.62	$15,600,759.95	$86,507,488.57	$22,958.46	3,768	1,486
South Dakota	$5,712,923.39	$686,932.13	$6,399,855.52	$16,161.25	396	175
Tennessee	$50,621,555.88	$13,993,951.06	$64,615,506.94	$20,512.86	3,150	1,077
Texas	$1,325,875,765.26	$468,960,530.48	$1,794,836,295.74	$27,567.06	65,108	20,395
Utah	$942,899.43	$202,236.88	$1,145,136.31	$17,350.55	66	27
Vermont	$5,712,953.83	$1,323,304.01	$7,036,257.84	$21,257.58	331	133
Virgin Islands	$13,714,143.86	$24,171,345.01	$37,885,488.87	$46,887.98	808	294
Virginia	$281,880,147.26	$54,258,059.06	$336,138,206.32	$20,827.70	16,139	6,101
Washington	$86,791,060.88	$17,829,587.55	$104,620,648.43	$26,777.74	3,907	1,360
West Virginia	$92,557,791.85	$40,038,260.89	$132,596,052.74	$17,001.67	7,799	2,991
Wisconsin	$20,125,657.08	$4,758,741.43	$24,884,398.51	$17,055.79	1,459	624
Wyoming	$236,225.06	$32,264.07	$268,489.13	$9,588.90	28	12
Total	$9,332,687,006.11	$2,768,293,768.01	$12,100,980,774.12	$24,388.39	496,178	166,368

Source: U.S. Department of Homeland Security, Federal Emergency Management Agency.

Appendix B. Key Provisions in the Biggert-Waters Flood Insurance Reform Act of 2012

On July 6, 2012, President Barack Obama signed into law the Biggert-Waters Flood Insurance Reform Act of 2012[77] to extend funding for the NFIP to September 30, 2017. This legislation includes several key provisions:

Actuarial Soundness, Program Solvency, and Affordability

- Premium Rate Structure Reform and Affordability

    o Immediately eliminate pre-FIRM insurance premium subsidies on second properties, severe repetitive loss properties and properties that have incurred flood-related damage that exceed the fair market value of the property, and commercial properties that have undermined the financial stability of the program.[78]

    o Gradually phase in actuarial rates for structures newly mapped into special flood hazard areas.[79]

    o Increase in the annual cap on premium rate increases from 10% to 20%.[80]

    o Authorize a new way of defining "average loss year" when setting annual flood insurance rates that include catastrophic loss years and raise the cap on premium increases.[81]

    o Study the economic costs and benefits to taxpayers of providing flood insurance vouchers to lower-income property owners.[82]

- Privatization

    o Study of the capacity of the private reinsurance market to assume a portion of the NFIP insurance risk[83] and clarify FEMA's authority to secure reinsurance from the private market to minimize the probability that the program would need to borrow Treasury funds.[84]

    o Require FEMA to obtain reinsurance proposals to lay off a portion of the risk.[85]

---

[77] P.L. 112-141, 126 Stat. 916.

[78] Id., Sec. 100205.

[79] Ibid.

[80] Ibid

[81] Ibid.

[82] Ibid, Sec. 100236.

[83] Ibid, Sec. 100232.

[84] Ibid.

[85] Ibid.

- o Require the Director of the Federal Insurance Office (FIO) to study and report to Congress on the claims-paying capacity of the private insurance market for natural catastrophic insurance in the United States.[86]

- Program Solvency and Debt Forgiveness

  - o Create a $12 billion catastrophe reserve fund to more effectively spread overtime losses from catastrophe loss years over time while reducing the likely need for borrowing from the Treasury. [87]

  - o Authorize FEMA to create a repayment schedule for funds borrowed from the Treasury.[88]

Flood Map Accuracy

- Establish a Technical Mapping Advisory Council (TMAC) to advise the administrator of FEMA on risk-based approaches to assessing future flood risk vulnerability[89] and an independent appeals board, Scientific Review Panels, for homeowners and communities to challenge revisions to their FIRMs with conflicting technical and scientific data.[90]

- Establish a process for communities to request a remapping based on standards developed by the TMAC and adopted by FEMA.[91]

- Establish a Federal Protection Structure Accreditation Task Force to better align the data that the U.S. Army Corps of Engineers collect during levee inspection with the data required under FEMA's accreditation program.[92]

- Establish a process and formula (COASTAL —Consumer Option for an Alternative System to Allocate Losses) for settling wind-related versus water-related property damage claims disputes by using scientific data currently collected by the National Oceanic and Atmospheric Administration (NOAA), academic institutions, and private entities, in conjunction with engineering formulas to be developed by FEMA, to help allocate total losses between the two perils or causes of loss after a major storm.[93]

Mitigation Funding Program Reform

- Combine and streamline FEMA's flood hazard mitigation programs and move toward risk-based mitigation planning and activities that result in sustainable action that reduces risk to life and property from floods.[94]

---

[86] Ibid., Sec. 100247.

[87] Ibid., Sec. 100212.

[88] Ibid., Sec. 100213.

[89] Ibid., Sec. 100215.

[90] Ibid., Sec. 100218.

[91] Ibid., Sec. 100216.

[92] Ibid., Sec. 100218.

[93] Ibid., Sec. 100253.

[94] Ibid., Sec. 100225.

NFIP Management and Operational Efficiencies

- Impose civil penalties or enforcement actions for non-compliance with mandatory flood insurance requirements.

- Set procedures for monitoring contracts and claims records.

- Require federal agencies to work together and share data to improve flood mapping.[95]

- Authorize a study of ways to improve interagency and intergovernmental coordination of flood mapping.[96]

---

[95] Ibid., Sec. 100220.

[96] Ibid., Sec. 100221.

Appendix C. Chronology of Public Laws That Reauthorized the National Flood Insurance Program: 2008-2012

Presidential Signing Date	Public Law	Last Day of Effective Program Authority	Lapse in NFIP Authority
September 30, 2008	P.L. 110-329; 122 Stat. 3575 H.R. 2638 (Price)—Consolidated Security, Disaster Assistance, and Continuing Appropriations Act, 2009 (Sec. 145)	March 6, 2009	
March 6, 2009	P.L. 111-6; 123 Stat. 522 H.J.Res. 38 (Obey)—Continuing Appropriations Resolution, 2009	March 11, 2009	
March 11, 2009	P.L. 111-8; 123 Stat 988 H.Res. 184 (Obey)—Omnibus Appropriations Act, 2009	September 30, 2009	
October 1, 2009	P.L. 111-68; 123 Stat 2047 H.R. 2918 (Wasserman Schultz)—Legislative Branch Appropriations Act, 2010 (Sec. 129)	October 31, 2009	
October 28, 2009	P.L. 111-83; 123 Stat. 2142 H.R. 2892 (Price)—Department of Homeland Security Appropriations Act, 2010	October 31, 2009	
October 30, 2009	P.L. 111-88; 123 Stat. 2904 H.R. 2996 (Dicks)—Department of the Interior, Environment, and Related Agencies Appropriations Act,2010 (Sec. 102)	December 18, 2009	
December 19, 2010	P.L. 111-118; 123Stat. 3409 H.R. 3326 (Murtha)—Department of Defense Appropriations Act, 2010 (Sec. 1005)	February 28, 2010	March 1, 2010
March 2, 2010	P.L. 111-144; 124 Stat 45 H.R. 4691 (Rangel)—Temporary Extension Act of 2010 (Sec. 8)	March 28, 2010	March 29, 2010
April 15, 2010	P.L. 111-157; 124 Stat 1116 H.R. 4851 (Levin)—Continuing Extension Act, 2010 (Sec. 7)	May 31, 2010	June 1, 2010
July 2, 2010	P.L. 111-196, §2(a); 124 Stat 1352 H.R. 5569 (Waters)—National Flood Insurance Program Extension Act	September 30, 2010	
September 30, 2010	P.L. 111-250, §2(a); 124 Stat 2630 S. 3814 (Vitter)—National Flood Insurance Program Extension Act of 2010	September 30, 2011	October 1, 2011
October 5, 2011	P.L. 112-36 §130; 125 Stat. 390 H.R. 2608 (Graves)—Continuing Appropriations Act, 2012	November 18, 2012	
November 18, 2011	P.L. 112-55; 125 Stat 710 H.R. 2112 (Kingston)—Consolidated and Further Continuing Appropriations Act, 2012, Div. D (Sec. 101)	December 16, 2011	

Presidential Signing Date	Public Law	Last Day of Effective Program Authority	Lapse in NFIP Authority
December 16, 2011	P.L. 112-67; 125 Stat. 769 H.J.Res. 94 (Rogers)—Making Further Continuing Appropriations for Fiscal Year 2012, and for Other Purposes	December 17, 2011	
December 17, 2011	P.L. 112-68; 125 Stat. 770 H.J. Res (Rogers)—Making Further Continuing Appropriations for Fiscal Year 2012, and for Other Purposes	December 23, 2011	
December 23, 2011	P.L. 112-74, Div. D, Title V, §573; 125 Stat. 985 H.R. 2055 (Culberson)—Consolidated Appropriations Act, 2012	May 31, 2012	
May 31, 2012	P.L. 112-123; H.R. 5740 (Biggert)—National Flood Insurance Program Extension Act	July 31, 2012	
July 6, 2012	P.L. 112-141; 112 Stat. 916; Div. F, Title II, H.R. 4348 – Biggert-Waters Flood Insurance Reform Act of 2012	September 30, 2017	

Source: Congressional Research Service.

Author Contact Information

Rawle O. King
Specialist in Financial Economics and Risk Assessment
rking@crs.loc.gov, 7-5975